Farm to Table

Grains and Cereals

ANN O. SQUIRE

Children's Press®
An Imprint of Scholastic Inc.

Content Consultant
Anuradha Prakash, PhD
Professor, Director, Food Science Program
Chapman University
Orange, California

Library of Congress Cataloging-in-Publication Data
Names: Squire, Ann, author.
Title: Grains and cereals / by Ann O. Squire.
Other titles: True book.
Description: New York, NY : Children's Press, an imprint of Scholastic Inc., 2017. | Series: A true
   book | Includes bibliographical references and index.
Identifiers: LCCN 2016025109| ISBN 9780531229323 (library binding) | ISBN 9780531235515 (pbk.)
Subjects: LCSH: Grain—Juvenile literature. | Grain—Growth—Juvenile literature. | Grain—
   Development—Juvenile literature. | Genetically modified foods—Juvenile literature.
Classification: LCC SB189 .S64 2017 | DDC 633.1—dc23
LC record available at https://lccn.loc.gov/2016025109

Front cover: A child carrying a
pitchfork through a field
Back cover: A baker with fresh bread

Find the Truth!

Everything you are about to read is true *except* for one of the sentences on this page.

Which one is **TRUE**?

T or F Cereals are sometimes used in nonfood items, such as soap.

T or F All grains are processed in the same way.

Find the answers in this book.

3

Contents

THE **BIG** TRUTH!

Insect Pests

Maize weevil

Refined flour (far left) and whole wheat kernels

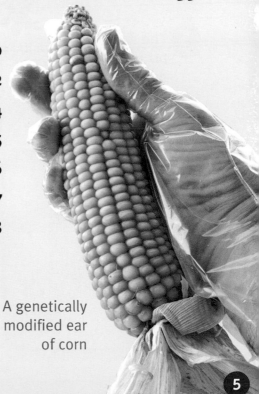
A genetically modified ear of corn

1 The soil is tested to make sure it can support healthy crops.

2 The soil is tilled and fertilizers are added. Seeds are planted, usually by machine.

From Farm

9 The flour or other product is packaged and sent to supermarkets and factories.

8 If flour is produced, it may be bleached and enriched with vitamins and minerals.

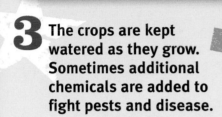

3 The crops are kept watered as they grow. Sometimes additional chemicals are added to fight pests and disease.

4 When the grain is mature, it is harvested. Depending on the cereal, a machine called a combine might be used. It cuts the cereal and separates the grains from the inedible parts.

o Table

5 The grains are stored in a cool, dry place.

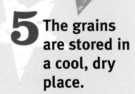

7 The grains are milled, or processed, and may be refined to remove the bran layer.

6 The grains are transported to the mill, where they are cleaned.

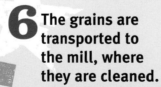

Many people add fruit and other toppings to their morning oatmeal.

Where Does Your Food Come From?

What do you usually eat for breakfast? A bowl of oatmeal? Eggs and a slice of toast? Maybe an adult in your house makes you pancakes, waffles, or French toast. For many people, breakfast consists of bread, **cereal**, or other **grain**-based foods. Did you ever wonder where these breakfast treats come from? How are they made? How different are they from the grains that go into them?

Grains have been an important part of human diets for thousands of years.

Ancient Cereals

The cereal in your breakfast bowl is made from wheat, corn, oats, or other types of grain. The bread in your sandwich might include rye, barley, or millet. These are all examples of cereals and the grains they produce. Cereals are grasses that are grown for food. Grains are the seeds of these cereals. Humans have been growing cereal crops and eating their grains for thousands of years.

This ancient Egyptian image shows workers planting and harvesting wheat.

People domesticated wheat in southwestern Asia more than 10,000 years ago.

Grain seeds are called kernels. They contain all the nutrients necessary to nourish a sprouting cereal plant. Whole grains also provide people with fiber, carbohydrates, protein, and important vitamins and minerals that keep us healthy. Grains are tough and durable so they last from season to season. This means people can store harvested grain for long periods before it spoils.

People check barley kernels for quality.

A Nearly Perfect Food

In many ways, grains are the perfect food. But there is a drawback. Unlike fruits or vegetables, raw grains cannot be digested. The hard coating that protects the grain kernel is too tough for our bodies to break down. In addition, our bodies cannot use the nutrients found inside grain kernels unless they have been processed.

Processing Grain

Our ancestors realized that, to make grain edible, they would have to process it in some way. After harvesting the mature, or ripe, grain, they used flat rocks to crush and grind the kernels. This broke down the tough outer coating, called the bran. The coarse, ground grains were mixed with water to form a dough or porridge, which was cooked. People could then digest the grain and absorb the nutrients.

Ancient people sometimes used millstones to grind grain. They put the grain between two large stones and rotated the upper stone, crushing the grain against the bottom stone.

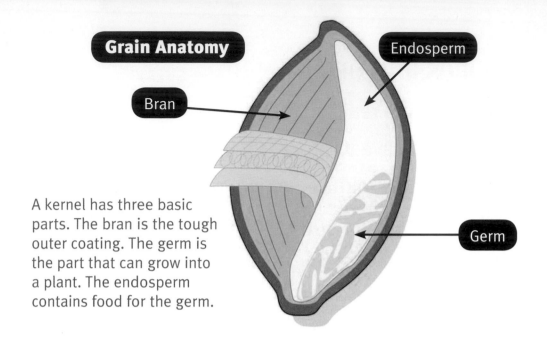

Grain Anatomy

Bran

Endosperm

Germ

A kernel has three basic parts. The bran is the tough outer coating. The germ is the part that can grow into a plant. The endosperm contains food for the germ.

One drawback to processing grains in this way is that they do not keep as well afterward. This is because the **germ** inside the kernel contains oil. When the kernel is ground, the germ is exposed to air and the oil quickly turns rancid, or spoils. This makes the ground grain taste bad. Ancient people only processed enough of the grain that they grew to last them a short time, so spoilage wasn't a problem. Today, however, grains are often stored a long time after being processed.

Making Breakfast Cereal

The flakes, crisps, and Os you might eat for breakfast are different from the watery porridge our ancestors ate. Today, flour or grain pieces are cooked with water, sweeteners, flavorings, salt, food coloring, vitamins, minerals, and preservatives. Machines form this mixture into flakes, puffs, or other shapes. Then the cereal may be coated with frosting. Marshmallows, nuts, or other ingredients may be added before packaging and reaching your breakfast table!

Growing Cereal Crops

In ancient times, people grew just enough grain for themselves and their communities. They planted the seeds by hand, used knives or **scythes** to harvest the mature crops, and ground the grain in small batches. Since then, people have come to depend on grains more and more. Today, growing and processing grain to feed the world's communities is big business.

Different types of wheat are harvested at different times of year.

Common Crops

Corn and wheat are the two biggest cereal crops in the United States, followed by **sorghum**, barley, and oats. Every year, U.S. farms produce more than 13 billion bushels of corn and more than 2 billion bushels of wheat. One bushel is about the same size as 8 gallons of milk. Because of the huge volume of grain, it is impossible to plant, harvest, and process the grain by hand. Every stage of the process is mechanized. Let's take a look at how wheat goes from seed to storage.

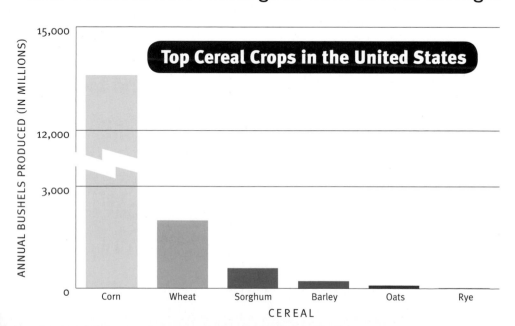

A tractor pulls a seed drill through a field.

Wheat: It Starts With the Soil

Before planting, the soil is tested to make sure it has the minerals needed for a crop such as wheat to grow healthy and strong. Then the top layer of soil is loosened, or tilled. **Fertilizer** may be added to the soil, too.

Seeds are sometimes treated with **pesticides** to control insect pests and with other chemicals to prevent disease. Then a tractor pulls a machine called a seed drill, which spreads the seeds evenly over the ground.

A machine called a sprayer is used to spray pesticides through a wheat field.

The wheat usually needs to be watered as it grows, to keep the soil moist. It is sometimes necessary to spray the wheat during the growing season to kill pests. As the wheat matures, the plant loses moisture and turns from green to brown. Then it is ready for harvest.

Farmers harvest wheat using huge machines called **combines**. They drive these machines through the fields. The combines both cut the grain and thresh it. Threshing consists of separating the edible kernels from the **chaff**, the plant's inedible stalks and leaves. The combines use large fans to blow the chaff away. The wheat kernels are then funneled into a collecting tank.

Combines allow a farmer to harvest large areas of land quickly.

Grains are often stored in large bins called silos.

Harvested grains need to be properly stored. Too much moisture will cause the kernels to rot or begin sprouting. To prevent that, freshly harvested wheat is placed in special bins to dry. Then it is transferred to large storage containers that have been cleaned thoroughly. Sometimes the containers or the top layer of grain is sprayed with pesticides. Heat can also damage the grains and encourage insects, so the wheat is generally stored in a cool place.

Where Do U.S. Grains Grow?

The United States is one of the top grain-producing countries in the world. Cereal agriculture is particularly important to the midwestern United States, where most of the country's grains are grown. Iowa grows the most corn, Kansas the most sorghum and wheat, and South Dakota the most oats. Most U.S. rice grows in Arkansas. North Dakota and Idaho are tied for the title of biggest barley-growing state.

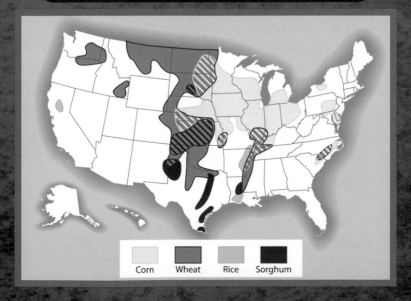

Major Areas of U.S. Grain Production

Corn   Wheat   Rice   Sorghum

Insect Pests

Insects are one of the biggest threats to cereal crops. Some pests prefer one crop over others, and some attack a plant at a particular stage of development.

Maize Weevil

MAIZE WEEVIL

The maize weevil attacks all kinds of grain, but its favorite is corn. It infests the kernels both before harvest and during storage. A female adult maize weevil drills a tiny hole in the kernel and lays an egg inside. When the egg hatches, the **larva** feeds on the inside of the kernel. After growing into an adult, it chews a hole in the kernel and escapes.

Rice Weevil

Flour Beetle

RICE WEEVIL AND GRAIN BORER

Rice weevils and grain borers are very similar to maize weevils. Despite their name, rice weevils feed on a range of grains, from rice and wheat to rye and barley. Grain borers have similarly varied tastes.

FLOUR BEETLE

Other beetles attack only when the grain is in storage. Flour beetles feed on grain dust and broken kernels. The females lay hundreds of eggs throughout the grain. Some flour beetles release a foul-smelling substance when they are disturbed. This makes the grain or flour unfit for consumption.

Grain Borer

CHAPTER 3

Processing: From Grain to Flour

Cereal grains must be processed before we can eat them. Depending on how they are processed, cereals can be turned into a range of products. Wheat may be turned into flour or baked goods, and oats into oatmeal. Corn is used in breakfast cereals, corn syrup, animal feed, fuel, and many other products. For a general idea of how grain processing works, let's trace the steps wheat follows after harvest.

Wheat flour is used in bread, pastries, cookies, and many other treats.

To the Mill

Railcars or trucks deliver the wheat grains to a mill. There, the grain is cleaned to remove stones, straw, and other debris. Moisture is added so the kernels' parts separate easily. Roller mills crush the kernels and remove the germ and, usually, the bran. Refined flour goes through several passes of this process and a final sifting. This results in white flour that includes only the kernels' endosperm. Whole or unrefined flour keeps the bran.

Rollers are big machines that can process a lot of grain quickly.

Refined flour (left) looks very different from unprocessed wheat kernels.

Bleaching and Packaging

After milling, flour is sometimes allowed to age. It is stored where it can be exposed to air for days or weeks. This improves its baking qualities. This is generally how flour was produced many years ago. Modern milling methods, however, speed this process with chemicals. These chemicals condition the flour for use in baking and make the flour whiter and brighter. This is called bleaching.

Removing the bran to produce refined flour strips the flour of many important nutrients. To replace some of what was lost, mills "enrich" the flour by adding iron and vitamins.

Some of the finished flour is packaged for sale directly to consumers at stores. Another portion is sent to factories. There, it is transformed into various foods, from bread to breakfast cereal.

Bread and pastries (left) are examples of food products that use grains. Bread is made from flour (right).

Rolled oats (left) and steel-cut oats (above) produce slightly different oatmeal textures.

Like wheat, corn and rye are often milled into flour. Corn is also dry milled to make grits and animal feed. Grains can be cracked or cut. Some oats used in oatmeal are rolled flat, but others are steel cut into small, hard pieces. Rice is sometimes parboiled. This means it is boiled or soaked in hot water before being milled. This moves most of the kernels' nutrients from the bran into the endosperm. This makes the refined rice more nutritious.

Wheat and other grains are sometimes sprouted. Sprouted grains start growing—or sprouting—a new plant before going through the mill. Puffed grains are usually steamed under high pressure. This makes the kernels expand, or puff up. Puffed rice is used in rice cakes and many cold breakfast cereals. Another puffed grain you probably know is popcorn.

Puffed rice is often used to make sweet treats.

The Many Uses of Corn

Corn has a huge variety of uses. Corn flour, cornmeal, and corn syrup are used in countless different foods for both humans and animals. Parts of the kernel are also used in soap, medicines, makeup, and even pencil erasers. The plant's inedible stem, husk, and cob may be found in paint, filling material, fuel, and many other products. In fact, fuel is the largest use of corn in the United States!

CHAPTER 4

Eating Right

Grains are an important part of diets around the world. Rice is a **staple food** throughout Asia. Wheat and corn are important across the Americas, Europe, and Africa. You probably eat grains with nearly every meal! As with any food, grains should be eaten in moderation, which means you shouldn't eat too many. Balance grains with fruits, vegetables, and other foods. You should also eat whole grains rather than refined grains for their fiber, vitamins, and minerals.

Thirty-five different cereal crops are grown around the world.

Finding the Nutrients

Grain processing is useful but not perfect. Refined grains can be stored a long time. Milling also gives grains a finer texture by removing the tough layer of bran. However, removing the bran makes the product significantly less nutritious. Whole, or unrefined, grains contain the endosperm and the nutrient-rich bran.

Timeline of Grains and Cereals

28,000 BCE

Early humans leave the first evidence of baking bread.

10,000 BCE

Humans first begin farming crops, including cereals.

8,700 BCE

Corn is first domesticated.

Enriching refined grains with added nutrients helps make them more nutritious. Today, nearly all the flour you find at the supermarket or in the packaged food you eat is enriched in some way. However, even enriched flour is less healthy than other grain options, particularly whole grains. This is because fiber is not added back in. Your body needs fiber to help it process food.

1894 CE
Companies produce the first corn flakes.

1957
Researchers make the first high-fructose corn syrup, a corn-based sugar substitute.

2,000 BCE
People in China cook the first known noodles.

Whole Grains

Eating whole grains helps keep your heart healthy, control your weight, and process waste in the body. Whole grains also fight diabetes, a disease in which the body cannot control the level of sugar in the bloodstream. They may even reduce the risk of certain forms of cancer. Whole grains—which are the best parts of a cereal—are a great addition to your meal! ★

Rice and other grains are an important part of a balanced diet.

Making Modifications

Cereals have changed since our ancestors first began farming them. For example, ancient people once grew teosinte, a cereal with narrow ears of small, hard grains. Through years of trial and error, they developed a plant with larger, more easily digestible kernels: corn. Today's scientists can change, or modify, a plant's **genes** to affect how it will grow, look, or taste. This genetically modified organism (GMO) might be designed to survive drought, fight off insect pests, or just taste better. However, not everyone is in favor of GMOs. Scientists are still studying them.

GRAINS AND YOU!

You can make grains a healthy part of your daily diet. The best way to do that is to look for whole grains. But where can you find them?

FROM BREAKFAST TO SNACKS

Oatmeal, either steel cut or rolled, is a good way to start your day. Do you like popcorn? It's a whole grain, too! The healthiest popcorn options have little or no added butter, salt, or artificial (fake) flavors.

SUBSTITUTE

If you like rice, try eating brown rice instead of white. White rice is only the grain's endosperm. Brown rice, on the other hand, includes the whole grain. You can also try wild rice. Though it's not really a member of the rice plant family, wild rice is a good whole-grain alternative. Quinoa is another delicious whole grain you can use to replace rice or pasta.

CHECK LABELS

When you buy packaged food— whether it's bread, boxed cereal, pasta, or other grain-based items— check the ingredients. These are listed on the food's nutrition label. Look for any of the whole grains listed below. The higher these are in the label's ingredients list, the better!

- Any cereals listed as "whole" or "whole grain," including corn, oats or oatmeal, rye, barley, and wheat
- Buckwheat
- Triticale
- Bulgur
- Millet
- Sorghum

Are GMOs Good or Bad?

People have long debated whether GMOs should be used as food. Some people argue that GMOs may not be safe for us or for the environment. Others point out that they could reduce the need for chemicals and increase the amount of crops harvested.

Which side do you agree with? Why?

Yes GMOs should be used!

Earth's population is growing rapidly. **GMOs can help make sure we grow enough food for everyone.** One type of GMO corn is called Bt corn. It can survive pest infestations without chemicals. This results in healthier plants, and farmers have bigger harvests. Other GMO varieties can tolerate chemicals that kill weeds, making it easier to spray the farm, so farmers save money. Bigger harvests and cheaper production costs lead to lower food prices. This means people can more easily afford to eat. Additionally, some GMOs in development, such as golden rice, are more nutritious than normal rice.

   Several studies have found no evidence of GMOs harming the health of people or animals. In some ways, GMOs may even be safer than non-GMO crops. Since GMO plants need few pesticides, farmworkers are exposed to fewer dangerous chemicals. GMOs are too beneficial to ban!

No GMOs should not be used!

Much of the money made from GMOs goes to big companies, not individuals who run their own farms. Some GMO plants are sterile, which means they cannot produce new plants from their seeds. This means that farmers must purchase new seeds each year from the companies that make them, such as Monsanto. These seeds can be very expensive.

   GMOs can also cause problems for the environment. The genes that give them some of their special abilities can be passed to other plants. Some weeds have developed the same hardiness and chemical resistance as GMO crops. This makes the weeds much harder to kill, and farmers end up using even stronger chemicals. We should ban GMOs!

True Statistics

Number of loaves of bread that could be baked from the wheat produced each year in Kansas: 36 billion

Number of kernels in a bushel of wheat: 1 million

Number of different uses for corn products: 3,500

Number of kernels on an ear of corn: About 800, arranged in 16 rows

Percent of oat harvest that is consumed by humans: 5

Percent of oat harvest that is consumed by livestock: 95

Percent of packaged foods in North America that contain GMOs: 70 to 80

Did you find the truth?

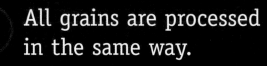

T Cereals are sometimes used in nonfood items, such as soap.

F All grains are processed in the same way.

Resources

Books

Bence Reinke, Beth. *The Grains Group*. Mankato, MN: The Child's World, 2013.

Lassieur, Allison. *Grains*. Mankato, MN: Amicus High Interest, 2015.

Markham, Brett L. *Mini Farming: Self-Sufficiency on 1/4 Acre*. New York: Skyhorse Publishing, 2010.

Visit this Scholastic Web site for more information about grains and cereals:

★ www.factsfornow.scholastic.com
Enter the keywords **Grains and Cereals**

Important Words

cereal (SEER-ee-uhl) a grain crop grown for food, such as wheat, corn, rice, oats, and barley

chaff (CHAF) the seed coverings and other debris that are separated out during threshing

combines (KAHM-bynz) harvesting machines for cutting and threshing grain in the field

domesticated (duh-MES-ti-kate-id) adapted to be grown and used by humans

fertilizer (FUR-tuh-lize-ur) a substance used to improve the soil so plants grow better

genes (JEENZ) the parts of a cell that control or influence the appearance, growth, and other aspects of a living thing

germ (JURM) the part of a grain that can grow into a plant and contains much of the grain's nutrients

grain (GRAYN) the seed or fruit of a cereal plant

larva (LAHR-vuh) an insect at the stage of development between an egg and a pupa, when it looks like a worm

pesticides (PES-tuh-sidez) chemicals used to kill pests, such as insects

scythes (SYTHZ) tools with a long handle and a large, curved blade used for cutting grass or crops by hand

sorghum (SOAR-gum) a cereal crop that is a major source of grain and feed for livestock

staple food (STAY-puhl FOOD) any food or product that is used regularly and kept in large amounts

Index

Page numbers in **bold** indicate illustrations.

About the Author

Ann O. Squire is a psychologist and an animal behaviorist. Before becoming a writer, she studied the behavior of rats, tropical fish in the Caribbean, and electric fish from central Africa. Her favorite part of being a writer is the chance to learn as much as she can about all sorts of topics. In addition to *Grains and Cereals* and other books in the Farm to Table series, Dr. Squire has written about many different animals, from lemmings to leopards and cicadas to cheetahs. She lives in Asheville, North Carolina.